HOW TO

BRAIN TRAIN

YOUR DOG

HOW TO BRAIN TRAIN YOUR DOG

This edition published in 2020

By SJG Publishing, HP22 6NF, UK

© Susanna Geoghegan Gift Publishing

Author: Helen Redding

Images used under license from Shutterstock.com

Cover design: Milestone Creative

Contents design: Jo Ross, Double Fish Design Ltd

ISBN: 978-1-911517-77-1

Printed in India

10 9 8 7 6 5 4 3 2 1

HOW TO
BRAIN
TRAIN
YOUR
DOG

Contents

INTRODUCTION 7

UNDERSTANDING HOW YOUR DOG'S BRAIN WORKS

What is brain training? 10

Does your dog need brain training? 12

Can any dog be brain trained? 14

How is your dog's brain wired? 16

Canine senses 18

Why does your dog like playing? 20

How do dogs learn? 22

The benefits of brain training: your dog 24

The benefits of braining training: you 27

Building a strong bond 30

Top dogs 32

GETTING STARTED

What do you need? 36

Treats and rewards 39

Fitting brain training in to your day 42

Encouraging playing 44

Training more than one dog 47

Clicker training 49

Be kind, be safe 52

LET THE GAMES COMMENCE!

First steps – top tips 58

Target training 60

Dinner time 63

Help around the house 66

Learning vocabulary: A, B, C 71

Counting games: 1, 2, 3 74

From the comfort of your chair 78

Games in the garden 82

Out walking 88

Home alone 93

The classics 96

DEALING WITH SPECIFIC PROBLEMS

Anxious dogs 104

Less active and older dogs 108

Help! It's not working! 113

TAKING IT TO THE NEXT LEVEL

Next steps: keeping your dog's brain stimulated 118

My dog is a genius! 121

Clever dogs: real-life stories 122

The future 126

Properly trained, a man can be dog's best friend.

COREY FORD

INTRODUCTION

You've probably heard of brain training for humans, and may have even tried it yourself. Remember those games and apps where you solved puzzles to keep your mind alert and stave off brain stagnation? Those may be gathering dust somewhere, but brain training is still part of our everyday lives – every time we do a crossword, memorise a shopping list or calculate the change we're due, we're exercising our brains.

Can you apply the same ideas to keep your dog stimulated, obedient and happy? Yes. You walk your dog to keep them physically fit – there's absolutely no reason why you can't exercise their brain too. (They've certainly got one – don't be fooled by the drooling, barking at random objects and the silly faces!) In this book, we'll explain how brain training works, and give you practical tips and ideas to share with your dog. It can be a lot of fun for both of you, and is an enjoyable way to interact and bond with your best friend.

Give it a go, and most of all, have fun – together. Who knows, maybe you'll discover you've got a canine Einstein at the end of the lead!

*You cannot share your life
with a dog ... and not know
perfectly well that animals
have personalities and
minds and feelings.*

JANE GOODALL

UNDERSTANDING
HOW YOUR DOG'S
BRAIN
WORKS

WHAT IS
BRAIN
TRAINING?

Brain training – we've all tried it, and may have even downloaded an app that promises to make our brains 20 years younger. Also known as cognitive training, the idea is to use mental exercises to flex and hone your cognitive skills in the way you'd tone your muscles in the gym. Brains can be trained to be smarter, fitter, faster and more responsive.

The skills normally targeted by brain training include:

- long- and short-term memory
- logic and reasoning
- sensory processing
- attention.

But that's just for humans, right? Wrong! It can be applied to anything with a brain. Well, within reason – possibly not a fly or a frog. But dogs, cats, apes, dolphins, elephants – even fish –are all capable of being trained to some extent. The brains of many mammals are surprisingly like the human brain, and dogs are no exception. There's a reason why training a puppy is very much like bringing up a baby or toddler.

This book will show you how to use the techniques of brain training to work with your dog and have some fun with them, while at the same time, keeping their brains in tip top condition. It will help you understand how your dog interacts with – and interprets – the world, and how you can work together to get the best out of each other. The more you understand how your dog functions, the better you will be able to cater for their needs and live harmoniously.

You'll also find out how to ensure that brain training your pooch is fun! If it stops being fun for either of you then abandon it. As a dog owner, your job is to be responsible and keep your dog safe, secure, happy and healthy. Brain training should be a fun and beneficial part of your toolbox for enjoying life with your canine best friend.

DOES YOUR DOG NEED
BRAIN
TRAINING?

As a means of mental stimulation and encouraging exercise, brain training can be beneficial to any dog. However, if you're concerned that your dog's brain isn't being used actively enough, then there are certain behaviours to look out for that give you the hint that Bonzo is bored rigid.

Lack of mental stimulation equals a bored dog, and the signs can be obvious. A bored dog will suffer from the following:

- weight gain (plus subsequent joint issues)

- excessive digging – remember how lovely your garden used to be?

- chewing – everything – read this as destructive behaviour generally

- seeking attention with excessive barking or whining when alone – attention seeking behaviour also manifests itself in your dog plonking itself on your lap and getting RIGHT IN YOUR

FACE – cute and endearing at first, but incredibly annoying if you're trying to do anything or watch TV

- raiding the trash ... or your laundry basket, the cushions on your couch or the pillows on your bed ...
- follows you around the house
- over-grooming and excessive licking
- obsessive tail-chasing – round and round and round and round ...
- listlessness – as humans, we know this symptom in ourselves well
- repeat escapes with the promise of adventure new sights and smells
- pacing the room and not sitting still.

If your dog is exhibiting any of the above behaviours, then you need to give them something to do right away. They're clever souls – just imagine how you'd feel if you had nothing to do. You'd probably start picking wallpaper off the wall and posting needy status updates on Facebook. That would leave you with broken nails and fewer friends.

Company and mental stimulation are no less important to dogs. You need to channel the energy your dog uses for mischief-making into healthy, positive behaviour. Play with them, run across fields with them and make sure they have toys to keep them occupied if you're out. And get stuck into some brain training! It won't be long before you can say goodbye to Bored Bonzo and hello to Brainy Buddy.

CAN ANY DOG BE
BRAIN
TRAINED?

Have you just looked at your dog and they've gazed back at you like there's nothing going on between their ears? They've cocked their head to one side, drooled a little and then yawned. You're wondering whether brain training is one step too far – maybe you should just both stick to playing fetch repeatedly. Have a bit of confidence in your dog and think again!

You know your dog's personality and how intelligent they are, regardless of how soppy and silly they can also be. Of course, brain training won't work perfectly with every dog, just as we humans click with some activities but not others. There will be dogs that are harder to work with, for example those with severe anxiety or who are suffering the aches and pain of old age – this book deals with different types of dogs who may find brain training tricky (but not impossible!) later. Some dogs will pick it up in a flash, and may even start teaching you a thing or two.

A puppy is perfect for soaking up new information and experiences. You can use their natural enthusiasm for playing to make the most of brain training. Interestingly, as their bodies aren't yet fully developed, puppies can find it hard to work off all their extra energy through physical exercise alone. Another way to tire them out is by stimulating their brain – games and puzzles are therefore excellent ways to ensure you have a content – and fast asleep – puppy at the end of the day.

There's absolutely no reason why you can't try brain training with a dog at any age. Dogs' brains are just like ours – soft and pliable, adapting to new information and capable of changing habits, given the right stimulation. Yes, it gets harder in the advancing years – that's why we have the phrases "You can't teach an old dog new tricks" and "Set in your ways". But mental stimulation should be an everyday part of your pet's life whatever their age, just as physical exercise is.

Some breeds of dog are much easier to deal with when it comes to obedience training, and the same applies to brain training. Labrador retrievers, German shepherds, poodles and border collies are considered to be some of the most intelligent dogs (see Top Dogs, page 32). If your pooch fits that bill, then you're probably in for an easier ride than other breed owners. But if you own an Afghan hound – which is considered to be one of the least intelligent breeds – don't despair. Patience is everything, and every owner of whatever breed needs oodles of it!

HOW IS YOUR DOG'S
BRAIN
WIRED?

To understand how brain training works, you need to understand your dog's brain. Dogs are amazing creatures – just think of the incredible work they do helping visually impaired people, sniffing out explosives and drugs and locating people missing in the rubble of buildings. But what makes dogs tick and how are they different to other animals, including us?

The structure of a dog's brain is very similar to that of humans and other mammals. Scans have shown that a dog's brain will light up in response to the same stimuli that human brains do. For example, dogs process human voices in the same way that we do. Part of their brain lights up when they hear a human voice, especially if it is an emotive sound like crying, which suggests they may experience similar emotions to us in reaction.

A dog's brain is a lot smaller than ours if you compare it to overall body size. The human brain is pretty huge, weighing in at around one-fiftieth the mass of the average human body. In comparison, dogs have a brain/body weight ratio of 1:125. Compare that to a horse's ratio of 1:600 and you'll get a sense of how clever dogs are!

Dogs have a level of cognition similar to that of an average two-year-old child, and some research says older, more like 4–5 years. Like young children, dogs can respond to voices and other stimuli, and can make associations (e.g. human + lead = walk). Try pointing at something and you'll see that your dog will look where you're pointing rather than at your hand. They also have a simple understanding of object permanence, so will know that something hidden hasn't just disappeared into thin air. With basic training, they can learn around 165 words and gestures (250 if they're a doggy genius). Dogs obviously can't speak (wouldn't it be great if they could?), but they do have a whole range of body language that they use to communicate with humans and other dogs. They can even count to 5 and perform simple calculations. Clever stuff.

CANINE
SENSES

Understanding how your dog's senses function will help you to understand how they engage in play and brain training. Humans are far more advanced at processing information and thoughts thanks to our highly developed prefrontal cortex, but dogs trump us in many ways.

SIGHT

Dogs have much bigger pupils and a higher ratio of rods to cones than humans, so they only need around one-fifth of the light that we need to see, giving them great low light vision. Whereas humans have 180 degrees of peripheral visions, dogs can have up to 250 degrees due to their lateral placement. They only see in shades of yellow and blue (not just black and white as most people believe).

HEARING

Dogs have amazing hearing. They can hear frequencies of up to 45kHz – humans can only hear up to around 20kHz. This means that the world can be quite a noisy place for your dog. If the frequency of a sound is over 36kHz, it can be painful for your dog and may cause barking or whining. And here's a great fact to share with your friends – did you know that dogs have over 18 muscles in their ears which allow them to be tilted, rotated, lowered and raised? This allows them to hone in to locate sounds precisely. But there's more – each ear can hear independently, so your dog has the ability to listen to two different sounds at once.

TASTE

When it comes to taste, dogs lag behind humans. The human tongue has 9,000 taste buds compared to just 1,700 in a dog's tongue. As a result, smell rather than taste is more likely to determine what your dog eats. If it smells good, they will eat it! Fortunately, dogs' taste buds have also evolved to know that if something tastes bad, it's likely to be harmful to them.

SMELL

Dogs use a much larger portion of their brain for analysing smells than humans do – the part of their brain that processes smell is 40 times bigger than yours. It's not surprising then that a dog's incredible sense of smell ranks above all its other senses. A dog's nose has 250 million smell receptors – compare that to the 5 million that you have! Amazingly, they can also move their nostrils independently, to determine the direction a smell is coming from. With one sniff, your dog can gather all kinds of information about the world around them.

WHY DOES YOUR DOG LIKE PLAYING?

Brain training your dog should be fun. It's all about playing mind games that can also get the four legs busy. Most dogs love to play, and it seems to be part of their make-up. Just think of how your dog's expression changes as you pick up a stick or a ball. It's the look of anticipation and excitement that children have, and that we sadly lose as adults. But why do dogs like playing so much?

For dogs, play has several functions:

- It helps them to learn motor skills like rolling, tugging and the level at which a bite stops becoming playful (a great way for a puppy to learn good manners).

- It trains them for the unexpected, e.g. what to do if they get knocked over or need to change direction rapidly, and how to deal with aggression from other dogs.

- It helps to build social relationships, not just with dogs but with humans, too.

Just as exercise and leisure time benefits humans, play is important for your dog's physical and mental health. It's an excellent way for them to express their natural behaviour. Energetic play will help combat weight problems – there's not just an obesity epidemic among humans, pampered pets suffer too. As joyful as their little hairy faces may look, play isn't therefore all about pleasure.

A 2018 study of 4,000 dog owners by Bristol University in the UK found that play is the key to a dog's happiness and well-being. The results showed that dogs who don't engage in a lot of play are likely to have behavioural issues such as anxiety and aggression. Making sure that your dog gets enough playtime will help to avoid any destructive and bad attention-seeking behaviour (such as whining and jumping up) that a bored pooch can develop.

How much time should you spend playing with your dog? Around 15 minutes a day is ideal to give them (and you!) a well-being boost and some stress-relief. But every dog is different, and you'll know when your own dog has had enough. Ever wonder why your dog is desperate to play but won't bring the ball back? Remarkably, dogs are very adept at prolonging games – they simply don't want the fun to stop. Even if playing tug of war with a rope could keep your dog entertained for hours, make brain training part of your dog's daily playtime – they'll find the variety stimulating.

HOW DO
DOGS
LEARN?

Understanding how your dog learns will better equip you to work with them most effectively as you explore brain training together. After all, it's no good telling them to "sit" in front of a textbook. In the wild, dogs would rely on their natural instincts (like any animal). Their behaviour would be geared toward survival. Although domesticated dogs don't lose all of their instinctive behaviours, they have to behave differently to function alongside humans. If a wild dog doesn't do it, then the behaviour is unnatural – i.e. learned.

How do they learn? They learn from other dogs, and of course, they learn from us. Think puppy training classes and those first desperate weeks trying to stop them running riot in their new home or not going berserk when meeting other hounds in the park. Plus, like us, they learn from trial and error.

Association is at the heart of a dog's learning process – that is, the consequences of their actions. It happens both through the way you teach your dog and their general interactions with the world around them. If a behaviour has a positive outcome (for example praise, rewards or simply getting what they want), then a dog will repeat it, anticipating the same result. Likewise, a negative outcome (for example, they approach a duck and it gives them a hefty peck on the nose) means your dog should hopefully avoid that action another time. Wouldn't it be wonderful if raising children was that simple?

This process of association is why repetition is so crucial to how your dog learns. Doing the same thing over and over and getting the exact same positive result cements the behaviour in your dog's mind. This is also why a dog owner's mantra must be "consistency in everything". So, if you're letting your puppy sleep on your bed, eat scraps from under the table and chase the delivery person but are then expecting them to miraculously stop this behaviour, well, you'll find you've made that proverbial rod for your own back. Undoing all those behaviours that you taught your dog were okay (albeit, through inaction), is mighty hard work.

THE BENEFITS OF BRAIN TRAINING: YOUR DOG

You wouldn't embark on a gym regime without knowing you were going to get something out of it would you? (Something other than an empty wallet and a bad back that is.) The same goes with brain training your dog. Yes, it's about having fun, but there are concrete benefits for your dog that will make your perseverance and shed loads of patience worthwhile.

WHAT WILL MY DOG GAIN?

Everything you've ever dreamed of since your dog graduated from puppy training! Okay, so that's probably going a bit too far, but it's not far off. Think about what irritates you most about your pet – it's probably not the endless hair and hoovering (as annoying as it is), but it is likely to be those moments when they don't obey your commands. Whether it's something simple like a command to come in from the garden, or something potentially dangerous like ignoring your warning not to run across a busy road, getting your dog to listen consistently can be hard work. Brain training will improve your dog's listening ability, perhaps in ways that conventional puppy training classes can't. When they can listen well, it will extend across everything you do with them.

Active and fun brain training games will also boost your dog's brain activity, and banish boredom. Not all dogs are lucky enough to have 24-hour one-to-one time with their owners. The reality of the world is that most people go out to work and have to leave their beloved hounds alone for part of the day. And then you come home to a shredded couch – ouch! (Hooray for the increasing number of canine-friendly workplaces.) If you can't give your dog 100% of your time, don't feel guilty about it. Brain training ensures that you give them brain stimulation when they need it to banish the boredom.

And if you need any more persuasion to give brain training a try, it can:

- increase your dog's overall movement and activity (so it is physically as well as mentally beneficial)
- raise their heart rate, just as we aim to at the gym
- allow dogs to better adapt to stressful situations – e.g. less fearful of new things
- increase their inquisitiveness
- help your dog to learn more quickly.

In fact, you can grow your dog's brain and make it more efficient! Introducing stimulating and brain-enhancing experiences helps build new neural pathways.

AND WHAT WILL THEY LOSE?

The simple – and very welcome – answer is this: unwanted and undesirable behaviour. Surely this is the dog owner's holy grail? Yes, but unlike a legendary ancient chalice, it's much easier to get your hands on. If you can work with your dog through brain training to improve their listening skills and mental fitness, then you can start to wave goodbye to digging, jumping up, unnecessary barking ... the list goes on. It will take hard work (and a whole lot of fun) but the results will be worth it. So, ask yourself, what have YOU got to lose?

THE BENEFITS OF BRAIN
TRAINING:
YOU

Owning a dog is a two-way relationship. You give an awful lot to each other in terms of love and companionship. In this mutual partnership, all of the great things you do for your dog will – hopefully – reap benefits for you too.

Although your dog learns an awful lot through engaging in brain training, you as an owner are being trained just as much. What can you learn in the process?

- How to read your dog's intentions and behaviour.

- How to communicate effectively with your dog.

- How best to convey instructions to your dog in order to get the response you want.

- How to control and ensure your dog's safety. If you master the basics, such as sit and effective recall, you can keep your dog out of trouble, and safe.

- Positive reinforcement is a huge part of any training, including brain training. Learn how it works and how to use it to get the best behaviour from your dog.

These are all incredibly useful skills for being a dog owner generally, not just in the context of brain training. Understanding the benefits above is especially important if you are a first-time dog owner. You cannot expect your dog to learn things by itself – the "going with the flow" or "whatever works" approaches are not recommended. For example, almost every dog trainer will confirm that positive reinforcement is the best way forward, especially with young puppies.

The principles behind brain training should become embedded in your mind as an owner. If this is the first time you've owned a dog, it will stop you from going down two unhelpful, undesirable and ineffective roads:

1. Getting your dog to do what you want through scaring them rather than encouragement. This will only result in your dog distrusting you and being anxious, and often also aggressive behaviour.

2. Love-bombing your dog without setting any boundaries. Dogs need structure and routine. Without that, you'll find that they rule the roost before you know it. It is of course vital to give dogs love and affection – but not without the rule-setting.

If you're at all skeptical about the benefits of brain training your dog, then at least start by opening your mind to the benefits that it has for you. You'll soon reap the rewards (and not in kibble form!) of having a dog that is happy, stimulated and keen to please.

BUILDING A
STRONG
BOND

The strength of the bond you build with your dog is incredibly important. It forms the basis of your whole relationship. Dogs are social animals, and like nothing better than to be with us. Once they leave their mother's side, you and your family become your dog's new "pack", and feeling part of that pack is essential to their socialisation. How can brain training help that process?

Obedience training is key. Unless your dog sees you as their trusted pack leader, you won't have any control. They must be prepared to listen to you and obey your commands, so if your dog isn't playing ball, you need to work on strengthening the bond between you to win their

respect. That's the call of the wild for you! Brain training can help you do this by providing a structure within which to co-operate and grow your understanding of each other.

Games are vitally important for a dog's development, for bonding with its pack of humans and socialising with unfamiliar dogs, as well as having fun. Dogs have a repertoire of games: running, chasing, play fighting wrestling and tug of war. They never seem to tire of playing the same old games – but after playing fetch with them two hundred times over the course of 10 minutes, you'll know that already. Introducing new brain training games can spice up your pet's life. The greater the variety of games you can share, the more enriching your time spent together will become.

If you want a happy dog, they need lots of company and attention (as well as plenty of exercise and a well-balanced diet). Dogs are happy if they are given all the things that they need. It's that simple! For example, research has shown that levels of oxytocin – the hormone connected to social bonding, and which the human body releases when we are in love – rise in dogs after they have been petted by their owners. Playing and engaging with each other is all part of this process, so make giving plenty of attention a regular part of your routine.

Understanding your dog's body language also will help you to build a strong bond of trust. Communication is key, so be consistent with your commands and rewards – your dog needs to know what is expected of them to feel secure. You'll hone these skills the more that you and your dog work at brain training games. When you can understand what your dog is trying to say – and vice versa – a whole new world opens up. By respecting your dog, you will find that your bond strengthens, making for a successful two-way relationship.

TOP
DOGS

It's not all that surprising, but research has found that some dog breeds are cleverer than others. Dogs bred to follow commands, such as collies and retrievers, are generally more intelligent than those dogs bred, for example, to hunt for the benefit of humans. No doubt many dog owners will fight the corner for their own pet's breed! Obviously, no individual dogs are the same, and they are clever in different ways. And it's very likely that there's a daft collie or two out there.

Is your dog in this top ten of the smartest canines?

1. Border collie – Very energetic (as a sheep-chasing working dog should be), affectionate and smart.

2. Poodle – Highly intelligent, poodles can be easily trained to track, hunt and retrieve. They were first used as retrievers in France.

3. German shepherd – Courageous, confident and smart. Brilliant working dogs and widely used as police dogs and service dogs.

4. Golden retriever – Intelligent, friendly and devoted. Great all-rounders whether hunting, serving as a guide dog or working in search and rescue.

5. Doberman pinscher – Strong, great stamina and speedy. Doberman pinschers are brilliant when trained as police or war dogs.

6. Shetland sheepdog – Playful, intelligent dogs that love learning new tricks. They're also great watchdogs because they have a tendency to bark at people.

7. Labrador retriever – Intelligent and gentle, and make excellent guide dogs and rescue dogs.

8. Papillon – Alert, friendly and happy. Fast and adaptable, they can be trained to do all sorts of tricks.

9. Bloodhound – Independent, inquisitive and friendly. Bloodhounds have been recognised for their scenting superpowers since the third century.

10. Rottweiler – Loyal, loving, confident and great guard dogs who love having a job to do. Well-suited to be service dogs, police dogs, herders and therapy dogs.

Don't be disappointed if your dog didn't make the list. The great thing about brain training is that it if it's done consistently and with lots of patience, your dog can – with your help – achieve so much. Remember, the aim of brain training isn't actually to make your dog the cleverest pup in the park. Its primary aim is to keep your dog's brain active, and contribute to their overall health and well-being. So even if your dog doesn't master everything, they are still benefiting greatly from the training.

*Dogs do speak, but only
to those who know
how to listen.*

ORHAN PAMUK

GETTING
STARTED

WHAT
DO YOU
NEED?

Think how lovely it is to start a new job with a new notebook and pen. Those small items placed neatly on your desk can provide you with a sense of confidence, and a feeling that you can achieve anything. Start brain training in a similar manner. You're not preparing for battle, you're preparing for a new adventure that promises brilliant benefits. What props and toys do you need to make brain training as effective, fun and easy as possible?

Gathering "equipment" doesn't need to cost anything. In yet another similarity between dogs and children, why buy expensive toys when an empty box will do? Have a look around the home for items that you can use for games:

• Any storage box/pot with a lid is perfect for seeking out games.

You can hide things to find in anything, even cardboard toilet rolls. Just make sure that what you use is safe to chew.

- A skipping rope – great for teaching body/eye co-ordination. Have a search of the internet for the video of Geronimo the dog skipping double Dutch!

- Good old paper cups are ideal for hiding a treat under.

- Recycle your old clothes. A strip of denim tied in a knot makes a great tug toy. You can also make a cheap but brilliant tug toy by plaiting strips of old t-shirt together.

- Pop some treats in an old shoe and seal it up with tape.

- You can fashion a treat dispenser from many household items – plastic bottles, cardboard tubes, plastic pipes. Use your imagination, but make sure it's safe for your dog.

Of course, if you want to spend some money, there plenty of dog "intelligence" toys on the market – from the simple to the fancy – that can help with brain games. For example,

- Dog puzzles. Yes, these are a thing! There are toys available that are specially constructed to include parts to slide and lift where you can hide treats.

- No dog should be without a kong – the leader of the toy pack.

- Knotted rope tuggers – millions to choose from, unless you opt to make your own (see above).

- Treat dispensers. Making it a challenge to access food and treats makes dogs have to think very, very hard.

- If you're planning on using clicker training, then guess what? You'll need to buy a clicker.

With all pet toys, whether homemade or shop bought, if you spot any damage or small pieces coming off, take the toy away from your pet in case it poses a danger to them. Playtime and brain training should always be supervised to ensure your dog is safe.

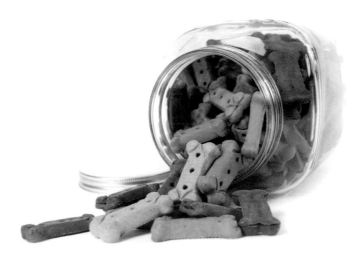

TREATS
AND
REWARDS

The way to a person's heart is through their stomach. Much the same can be said of dogs. Training your dog requires them to make a positive association between a particular behaviour and a reward. As much as a dog loves a good scratch and verbal adoration, nearly all dogs love an edible treat even more. Dogs don't do things to make us happy – they need a benefit for themselves. Quite mercenary really. So as you brain train your pooch, be prepared to pull a doggy snack out of your pocket every time you go in search for a tissue ...

The key rule to remember is that treats are to reinforce behaviour, and are not a form of bribery. Reward should come after an action has been completed and not as a way of encouraging your dog before they obey you. If you wave a snack under their nose as they run through slalom poles then of course they will follow! But will they do it when you're empty handed? So, keep those treats out of sight until it's time to say "well done".

"Isn't my dog going to get awfully fat?". No, not if you're ensuring they get plenty of physical exercise and recognise that reward-based training is only short-term. Treats are a great way to kick-start training and make those essential positive associations. However, as your dog gets good at responding, try to reduce the number of treats they get. Trainers recommend that when your dog responds 90% of the time, you should make the food rewards random and less frequent. Your dog won't unlearn what they've mastered with you – the positive association will stick.

WHAT MAKES A GOOD BRAIN TRAINING TREAT?

- Keep them small and easily swallowed. You don't want your dog settling down to a half hour chew when you're keen to get on with the next game. Pea-sized is perfect. For dogs, size really doesn't matter – what matters is that there are lots of them.

- The treat isn't going to work unless your dog finds it delicious. Ever tried rewarding a child with a carrot when they're looking at the ice cream tub? You know your dog, so you know what they like best and what will most motivate them.

- Have some treats to hand that are even more appealing than the ones you regularly use. There will be times when your dog needs just that little extra bit of motivation, particularly at times when lots is going on around them and concentration wanes. Whipping out that slice of sausage rather than a nugget of kibble might just be the reward they need to refocus.

Try not to over-reward your dog. It is easy to do when you love your best friend, and you're that delighted they've obeyed you. While it's important to use rewards regularly to reinforce actions and behaviours, too much of a good thing can become boring for your dog. Kibble can lose its va-va-voom! As soon as that happens, your dog loses their motivation and you're stuck. The simple answer is to reward regularly but not all the time. Keep it unpredictable and you'll find your dog working even harder for their reward. This applies even more so when you're maintaining good behaviour rather than training. You can keep using food treats, but minimise them and replace them with lots of rubs, scratches and play.

FITTING
BRAIN
TRAINING
IN TO YOUR DAY

Utter the words "brain training" and it can sound pretty full-on, like you're hothousing your dog to appear on a high-brow quiz show, or coaching them to take the Mensa test. Really, it's not that intense! Brain games should form part of your everyday interactions with your dog, just as a walk in the park or a grooming session do.

Try to set aside some time each day to do brain training. How much time is very much up to you — you know your dog best and how long they can stay focused for. Training of any kind with a dog that has become bored (or an owner who has become frustrated!) won't be effective. If all your dog can manage is 5 minutes a day, then go with that and gradually build it up if they seem amenable.

If boredom during the day is an issue with your dog, you may find it manifesting in destructive behaviour, for example chewing furniture. Try slotting in short brain training sessions throughout the day to alleviate that boredom and nip it in the bud before bad behaviour ensues. Again, you know your dog best – what works with other dogs may not work for them. Experiment with the time and frequency you spend playing brain games and you'll develop a picture of what is most effective.

You might find that combining games with one of your daily walks is a good way to remind yourself to engage your dog in some brain stimulation. Perfect if that works, but you may find that being out in the open is too much of a distraction. A throng of sounds, smells and sights is just what an inquisitive dog can't resist, sometimes even if treats are on offer! When starting out brain training, it might be a better idea to base yourself in your own home or garden. In a quieter, more familiar setting, a dog will find it far easier to concentrate and focus on the task in hand.

Any brain training is better than no brain training. But make sure that you do it when the conditions and the mood are just right. An eager and receptive dog plus a calm and patient owner are the key ingredients to success!

ENCOURAGING
PLAYING

For brain training to work, your dog has to be in the right mood to learn, and to play. Puppies love to play, but there is still an element of them needing to learn how to do it successfully. If you adopt a rescue dog that has never been exposed to toys and games, they might have no idea what to do if you throw a ball. If playing isn't completely instinctive, how can you encourage you dog to enjoy playing?

If your dog isn't used to playing then start off slowly. Don't overwhelm them with new toys and games – work on introducing new things gradually. When they do express an interest in something new, reward them so that you start to build positive associations with play. As long as your dog is comfortable, you can then start to really involve yourself in the games. Sit close to them and engage with them. It's a really good opportunity to bond too. You can even show them  how to play. Okay, so you might not be Andy Serkis, but you can probably do a rough imitation of a dog once you're past the "feeling silly" stage. Your dog needs to learn that not only are toys fun, but that you're fun too.

The ideal time to play is when your dog is excited. You'll learn to recognise when they're feeling playful. For example, it could be when they're bouncing up and down at the prospect of going out for a walk. Seize these opportunities even if it's just for a couple of minutes playing. It's a good idea to keep some toys in every room in your home so that no chances for a bit of fun are missed.

There are some common myths about playing with your dog that you may come across:

1. That you shouldn't mix play and training. Well, this book shows us that this is rubbish! The best training happens when your dog views an activity as a game rather than a formal lesson.

2. Only puppies want to play. Again, untrue! Play stimulates dogs mentally and physically, and they need that throughout their lives. For ideas on how to play with older dogs, see page 108.

3. Don't play tug. Some "experts" have suggested that playing tug creates aggressive behaviour in dogs. Actually, dogs learn an awful lot from playing tug. It teaches them about controlling their impulses and mouths, knowing when to "drop it" and how to co-operate.

If you play together regularly, your dog's love for play will grow. Always end your play sessions on a high note and make it your choice when to stop (not because you're forced to by a dog that's become overexcited and unruly).

TRAINING MORE THAN
ONE
DOG

Yikes! Brain training with one dog seems daunting, but what about if you've got two or more to deal with? Is it possible to do this without growing several extra sets of arms, or shipping in containers full of extra patience?

The simple answer is to train each dog separately. Sorry! Don't groan. Yes, that's more time and effort, but ultimately it will allow you to get the best results. The good news is that once you've trained each dog individually, you can start to bring them together to share the fun.

There are several reasons why it's hard to brain train dogs together:

- Think about sitting at the back of class with your friends – are you likely to be distracting each other or listening intently to the teacher? If you're honest, it's the former. Training requires a calm atmosphere in which your dog can focus, and introducing more dogs into the mix is likely to make it incredibly hard for your dog to give their undivided attention to the task in hand.

- What kind of relationship do your dogs have with each other? If they're very competitive, then that's another good reason why you should avoid attempting to train them at the same time. It can be particularly problematic if they compete over food as it will make reward-based brain training chaotic and potentially stir up aggression.

- Throughout, this book has stressed how brain training is a two-way process and should be fun for both you and your dog. Why make life hard for yourself by splitting your attention among your pack, as much as you love them all? Making life easy for yourself will reduce your potential frustration, and maintain an atmosphere of calm.

CLICKER
TRAINING

Sounds quite exciting doesn't it? Sadly, if you've got visions of pulling on some tap shoes and dancing your way to a brain trained dog then you're going to be sorely disappointed. Clicker training is far more mundane. It's another trick up a dog owner's sleeve (sometimes literally in this case) for encouraging actions and behaviour through positive associations.

A clicker is a nifty little device that does exactly what it says on the tin – it clicks when you press it. It's a simple and efficient gadget that can have a brilliant effect. When your dog is behaving in the way you want them to, click the clicker and immediately reward them with a treat. At first, the clicking sound won't mean anything to your dog, but with repetition, they'll become aware that the click triggers a reward – then they'll wonder what they were doing when they heard the click that earned them the reward. And finally, bingo! Rover will realise that desired behaviour equals click equals treat.

What's the secret behind the clicker? It's not rocket science. Your dog is so used to hearing you speak and the everyday noises surrounding them, that when they hear a new, unusual noise – a click – they prick up their ears and pay attention. The click breaks through all of the mundane babble that your dog is used to. Most importantly, for an animal driven by its stomach, it is a very appealing sound if it means a treat is coming.

Using a clicker does require you to be on the ball though. Your reflexes need to be on fire, so pay attention to exactly what your dog is doing. The click must come at exactly the right moment in order to create the association with the intended behaviour. As soon as the dog is doing what you want them to – not a moment before or a moment after – CLICK. Of course, it will take some practice and you'll get it wrong to start with, but persevere. Any kind of training is a learning curve for both you and your dog.

Clicker training teaches your dog to be creative and to take initiative. Your dog needs to try to get it right, and will make mistakes along the way before figuring it out. It's a brilliant way to teach them to be creative and improve their problem-solving skills – perfect for brain games.

But as you've read over and over in this book, don't assume that clicker training will be right for your dog. Perhaps they're not bothered by treats (yes really, this can happen) so clicks or indeed any reward-based training will fall on deaf furry ears.

BE KIND,
BE SAFE

If your dog's brain is being stimulated through play then in all likelihood they are having fun. And that's exactly how it should be. If it stops being fun, there's a risk it could stop being kind, even without you realising it.

How can you tell if your dog is unhappy? Reading your dog's body language will give you a good indication of how they are feeling. It's easy to recognise the body language of a happy dog. If your dog looks like he's smiling — mouth open, tongue sticking out a bit or lolling over the lower teeth, edge of the lips curled upwards — he probably is. Happy dogs hold their heads in a neutral position (neither thrust forward or turned anxiously away), the ears are also relaxed and without tension. The face and eyes look relaxed and the tail may be wagging gently from side to side.

Anxious body language is easy to spot too — your dog's body gestures will be slow and cautious, tail is lowered and may be tucked beneath the legs, ears are pushed back flat against the head, mouth is closed and tense, or else the dog may be panting excessively and/or licking its lips. Another sign of anxiety and uncertainty is when your dog raises their front paw – a shorter version of a bigger sign of submission. When a dog rolls onto his back in submission, he begins by raising the front paw and then rolling the front part of his body. Raising the paw is the first part of this procedure, so it expresses anxiety and uncertainty. You can reassure your dog by staying calm, smiling and saying relaxing phrases in a soothing voice, for example, "It's fine, everything's okay".

Brain training won't always go to plan. Your dog might have zero attention span on a particular day when even a passing ant

seems more interesting than you. If this happens, just leave it for the day or try again later. By persisting when your dog isn't in the mood, they'll soon pick up on your frustration. Avoid using their name with a negative tone or context. If they think you're angry with them or that there's a punishment on the way, they'll simply start ignoring you, compounding the problem. Never physically force them to do something – always show them. Last but far from least: losing your temper and shouting or punishing your dog is cruel, and it never works.

In terms of being safe, the section "What Do You Need?" (page 36) looks at the importance of keeping an eye on the toys you're using for brain training. Anything that gets damaged or starts to have small pieces break off from it needs to be kept away from your dog so that there's no danger of them swallowing anything. It's just a matter of common sense – and dog owners have oodles of that!

I've seen a look in dogs' eyes, a quickly vanishing look of amazed contempt, and I am convinced that basically dogs think humans are nuts.

JOHN STEINBECK

A dog is the only thing on Earth that loves you more than he loves himself.

JOSH BILLINGS

LET THE GAMES
COMMENCE!

FIRST STEPS
– TOP TIPS

So, today's the day you've decided to start brain training your beloved. Well done – you and your dog won't look back. You're about to see the positive benefits that enriching your pet's brain can bring. You understand how your dog's brain works, you've gathered the props and toys (see page 36) that you might need, and your pockets are brimming with treats (see page 39). How do you make a start?

- Find somewhere quiet for your very first session, therefore minimising any chance of distraction. If it's somewhere your dog is familiar with, that will help too.

- Don't overwhelm your dog in the first session. Start slowly and don't expect amazing results from your initial attempts. Introduce some simple games, making it as fun and relaxed as possible, and this will lay solid foundations for the next session.

- Start as you mean to go on. Always be consistent to avoid confusing your dog.

- Tempting as it is to become a sergeant major, don't change your personality. Training is not a serious assignment – it's supposed to be fun! If you adopt a harsh tone when training but your dog is used to you being affectionate, then they'll assume they've done something wrong before you've even got started.

- Don't feel awkward. In the way that some people struggle to play with children on the same level, you might initially feel a bit silly when you start brain training. There's no simple advice for this other than to get over it! Getting on to the same level as your dog is likely to make training far more effective, so swallow your pride.

- Don't forget the importance of patience. Just like humans, different dogs learn at different rates. Did you struggle with maths concepts at school? Just imagine how unhelpful it would have been if you'd got a clip round the ear every time you got an answer wrong. Compare that to the teacher who sat down with you to explain everything, and encouraged you to keep trying.

- End the first session with something really positive. Get your dog to do something they've already mastered, even if that's just following the "sit" command. Give them lots of praise and rubs, and they'll begin to associate this brain play time with feelgood emotions.

TARGET
TRAINING

Target training is a fun exercise to get started with. And no, neither you or your dog is the intended target! Target training really exercises your dog's brain by teaching them to touch a particular item with a part of their body. So, for example, you could teach your dog to ring a bell with its nose to say it wants to go out for a toilet-break, or you could teach them to sit on a particular blanket to stop them bothering you when you're cooking or eating.

BRAIN GAME: GET NOSEY

Aim of the game: When starting off with target training, think small and simple. Try teaching your dog to touch an item with its nose.

1. Find a target. Your hand is perfect to begin with, or perhaps a favourite toy.

2. Show the target to your dog, placing is about half an inch in front of its nose.

3. As soon as your dog pays attention to the target – even better if they touch it straightaway – give them a reward and lots of praise (and click your clicker if you're clicking).

4. Repeat step 3 if all's going well.

5. Once your dog has got the hang of the basics (remember this needn't be in the first session – it may take longer), try moving the target away a little further but not so far that it makes the change too difficult for your dog, or to a different position.

This is a fun game, so you may find that you dog gets a bit overexcited and tries to bite or snatch the target. If this happens, be patient and simply reward them as they move towards the target rather than when they've touched it.

BRAIN GAME: FOLLOW THE TARGET

Aim of the game: Once your dog has got the idea of a target, teach them to follow a target. This is particularly useful for getting them into cars, into their beds or off your favourite spot on the couch.

1. Start off by showing them the target. It needs to be a physical object you can move rather than your hand, so a toy will work well.

2. Hopefully your dog will move towards the target – as they do, move it slightly further away from them so that they have to reach for it. Reward and repeat until you've both mastered a short distance.

3. As both your and your dog's confidence grows, move the target a little bit further ... a little bit further ... a little bit further ... gradually building up the distance – don't forget the rewards. Again, don't expect to achieve this in one session.

4. Eventually, your dog will be happy to follow the target, and you can utilise the target's power! Gradually phase out the edible rewards and replace with lots of praise.

Is your dog refusing to follow the target? Are you remembering to reward and praise? In any brain training, this is key in the initial stages. If that's not the issues, then start from scratch again and

try to master the shorter distances. Take it even more slowly and you'll soon find that your dog takes the bait.

DINNER
TIME

How about making your dog work for their dinner at the same time as stimulating their brain? This sounds horrific to a human – just imagine ordering food in a restaurant and having to solve a cryptic crossword before you're allowed to eat. Gulp. Getting your dog's brain working at dinner time is a good way of efficiently working brain games into your day – you're going to be feeding them anyway so why not make it fun and stimulating? Slowing down the eating process, and therefore slowing down digestion, can also make for a happier and healthier dog – no more wolfing it down like a … well, like a wolf.

There are lots of interactive feeding toys you can buy that will add a puzzle element to dinner time. From "slow bowls" to a complex feeder that looks like the Death Star and also cleans your dog's teeth (yes, it's a thing), the choice can be quite overwhelming. Brain training at dinner and treat time doesn't need to be expensive – think about what you can do yourself to make it interesting and challenging.

BRAIN GAME: WHERE IS DINNER?

Aim of the game: To engage your dog's sense and tracking skills.

Okay, so this would be REALLY annoying if someone did this to you as a human. Rather than putting your dog's meal in the same place each day, try mixing it up for an extra challenge. You don't need to hide the food even, just put it somewhere other than its usual location. By encouraging your dog to hunt for its dinner, it will have to utilise its sense of smell and tracking abilities

BRAIN GAME: WHERE'S YOUR BOWL?

Aim of the game: Teach your dog to find something by name. This is a good game to play before meal times to add a bit of excitement (if your hungry dog needs it). Make sure that the bowl you use is easy for your dog to pick up, and that it won't break if it gets dropped.

1. Encourage your dog to take the bowl from you, and when they do, reward them with a treat.

2. Each time, let your dog hold the bowl for a little bit longer – still giving rewards. When you get the hang of this, encourage your dog to bring the bowl to you. Keep those treats coming!

3. The next step is to encourage your dog to pick the bowl up from the floor and bring it to you.

4. Start to introduce a prompt word so that your dog knows what you're expecting them to do – perhaps "dinner" or "hungry". They'll soon begin to associate that word with fetching the bowl and bringing it to you.

5. As with many brain games, it's about extending distances a little bit further each time. Increase the distance until your dog can bring you the bowl from the spot where they normally eat. And now you can start to share dinner time duties, and spare your back!

Help! Your dog is now so full of treats that they can't eat their dinner. This is a risk while you're training, so try not to train too close to dinner time even if it's a dinner related activity. Remember that it's a temporary issue because once your dog has mastered the game, you can withdraw the edible rewards.

HELP
AROUND
THE HOUSE

Wouldn't it be wonderful to have extra hands to help around the house? How about extra paws? It seems such a waste not to combine your dog's brain training with practical activities around the home that benefit the whole family. We're not talking doggy slave labour here, more that if your dog is part of the family, they really ought to contribute as part of the team!

BRAIN GAME: DOORBELL

Aim of the game: To teach your dog to behave appropriately and sit in a designated place when your doorbell rings. When your doorbell rings or there's a knock at the door, does your dog turn to look at you then just go back to what it was doing? The answer is probably no. Like many dogs, it will no doubt get very excited, start barking and whizz around like a mad thing. This game can take a little while to perfect, but is definitely worth it.

1. Choose the spot in which you'd like your dog to end up sitting when someone comes to the door. If they're good with visitors, that spot can be close to the door. If they're more anxious about people calling, choose a spot in a room where they can feel secure. Use a marker to flag where the spot is – maybe a blanket or a cushion.

2. Teach your dog to go to that spot, and reward them with a treat when they do.

3. Now you can start to introduce the doorbell. Chances are that your dog will immediately head for the door when they hear it. Wait for their attention to come back to you and call them back to their spot and reward them for sitting back down in the right place.

4. Repeat, repeat, repeat. Your dog will start to make that positive association between the doorbell ringing and being rewarded for sitting in the correct place.

5. And now the next stage – actually opening the door! Take it slowly and only reward your dog when they stay where they should be as the door opens.

BRAIN GAME: HOOVER IT UP

Aim of the game: To teach your dog to pick up rubbish and put it in the bin.

Okay, so this doesn't teach your dog to use a vacuum cleaner – wouldn't that be wonderful? – but you can get some help with tidying.

1. Start off by placing a piece of rubbish (e.g. some scrunched up newspaper) on the floor and sit near to it with your bin at the ready. Using your "retrieve" command, get your dog to pick up the paper and then encourage them to bring it to you and drop it into the bin. Cue their reward.

2. Repeat, and gradually add extra items at varying distances.

3. Your aim is to not have to be near the bin in order for your dog to deposit the rubbish. Of course, what you want to be doing is sitting in your armchair pointing out the items that you want your dog to retrieve and pop in the bin. Bliss!

BRAIN GAME: CLOSE THE DOOR

Aim of the game: To teach your dog how to push a door closed – basically so you don't have to get up and do it.

1. Your dog needs to know how to touch a target, so start off with "Target Training" on page 60.

2. Once they know how to touch a target, transfer that target to a spot on the door that is easily reachable for your dog. Obviously, it's preferable if the target you've trained with is something you can easily attach to a door, e.g. a post-it note or similar. You might have trouble attaching anything big or heavy! Encourage your dog to touch the target on the door with either their nose or paw, and reward them with treats and praise when they do.

3. When they push hard and the door moves, give them lots of extra praise. This will help them to associate closing the door with the behaviour that earns them the biggest reward.

4. Introduce the words "close the door" as a cue to accompany the action. The more you practice, the better your dog will get. They'll eventually be able to close the door for you without needing the target and by simply hearing you tell them to "close the door".

QUICK LIFE HACKS

Dogs love having a job to do. It keeps them both physically active and mentally stimulated. Here are some more chores you can easily teach your dog to help with:

- If your dog has learnt the names of everyone in your family, send them to wake up the late sleepers! See "Where's …?" on page 73. Your family will really love you for it.

- If you're always losing your keys, train your dog to find and retrieve them.

- Find and retrieve has lots of uses when you're doing the household chores. If you can teach your dog the names of objects, they can fetch them for you as and when you need them. Contemplating dusting? Have your dog bring you the feather duster. If you're prone to procrastinate then you'll no longer have the excuse that you can't be bothered to get your cleaning equipment. And when you're done, your dog can fetch your slippers and bring you your newspaper!

LEARNING VOCABULARY:

A, B, C

We know how smart dogs are. With specialist training, the cleverest dogs can learn up to 250 words and gestures (around 165 words with basic training). Amazingly, Chaser the Border Collie (search for her online) has a vocabulary of over 1,000 words – more than any other animal or species except humans. She can also understand sentences with multiple grammar components.

Not all dogs can achieve the same as Chaser, but teaching vocabulary is still a great brain boost. Although dogs self-teach vocabulary to some extent (by osmosis, if you like), putting your own effort in to teaching it benefits your dog by keeping them mentally challenged and stimulated. Plus, the more you can understand each other, the stronger your bond and the happier your relationship.

When trying to teach new words, as with any training, positive reinforcement and treats are the golden rule. Your dog simply won't learn if they are bored or don't understand what you are asking of them.

Dogs find it easier to understand concrete words that relate to things, rather than abstract concepts. If you give names to your dog's toys, they can associate a concrete word with those objects. If you teach a word like "hungry" you may think your dog is responding to an abstract concept, but really, they have learnt to associate the word with your taking a tin of dog food out of the cupboard. Here, it's the concrete thing not the abstract that they're responding to.

BRAIN GAME: NAME THAT THING

Aim of the game: To teach your dog to associate a name with an object. When you're teaching new vocabulary, don't overwhelm your dog. Start with one object at a time.

1. Choose an object such as a small blanket. The easiest way for your dog to learn a new word is to attach it to an action, so encourage them to find the blanket and bring it to you.

2. Repeat, repeat, repeat. The message will eventually get through that objects have names, and once your dog understands that, it will become easier to teach them more words.

3. Once they've learnt the name of several objects, you can start to make more of a game of it. Spread out a selection of toys – some your dog will know the names for, some they won't – and

ask them to find a particular one. This will challenge them to actually think about it, rather than just grab the one they most like the look of (which of course they will still do on occasion!).

BRAIN GAME: WHERE'S ...?

Aim of the game: To teach your dog the names of family members.

1. With the person nearby, ask your dog 'Where's ...?' and positively reinforce the question by looking swiftly in the right direction.

2. Keep repeating step 1 and keep the question consistent. Your dog will soon associate the name with the individual.

3. Move on to the next person!

The more words you teach your dog to associate with objects, the more they will grasp the concept, and the quicker they will therefore learn new words. It's a brilliant way to flex their brain muscles, and can be used to your benefit next time you settle down on the couch and realise you've left the remote control across the other side of the room.

COUNTING GAMES:

1, 2, 3

In 2009, research conducted into canine intelligence by animal psychologists in Canada revealed that dogs are as intelligent as an average two-year-old child. The research found that dogs can count to five and perform simple calculations. Clever stuff (plus your dog is probably better behaved than a toddler). Have a go at introducing your dog to numbers and see how far they can go.

BRAIN GAME: COUNT TO THREE

Aim of the game: As the game says on the tin, your dog will learn to count to three. Don't believe it? Give it a try.

For this game to work, your dog should be familiar with target training (see page 60) as they will need to touch the objects in the game with their nose or paw. What do you need? Find three items that look similar, for example three balls or three plastic cups. (You can use food as long as your dog can restrain itself from eating the props!) You'll also need three targets (for example, a coaster) labelled 1, 2 and 3.

1. Place one of your objects and the number 1 target on the floor, point at it and say "One". When your dog touches the target, reward them with a treat. Keep at this until your dog responds every time.

2. Repeat step 1 with the number 2 and number 3 targets (each alongside one of the objects).

3. Gradually stop pointing at the target and just say the number.

4. Once this is mastered, drop saying the number and let the dog choose the correct number target by just looking at the number of objects.

Yes, you're right, it does sounds tricky. But give it a go – and plenty of time – and you'll be surprised at what your dog can accomplish.

BRAIN GAME: COUNTING WITH BARKS

Aim of the game: This is a neat little trick that gets your dog thinking, and also looks pretty impressive to family and friends. To do this trick, your dog needs to know how to follow the hand signal to bark/"speak".

1. Start off by sitting facing your dog. Looking at your dog, hold a treat in your left hand, raise your right hand and ask your dog to bark. As soon as they bark, drop your hand, avert your eyes and reward them with the treat.

2. Repeat step 1, but only reward your dog after two barks.

3. Keep plugging away until your dog gets the drift that they need to keep barking until you drop your right hand and look away.

Now you and your genius mathematician dog can impress your friends with canine counting. Give your dog a simple calculation to do and let them bark the answer. Only the two of you will know that there's no actual maths going on!

A well-trained dog will make no attempt to share your lunch. He will just make you feel so guilty that you cannot enjoy it.

HELEN THOMSON

FROM THE
COMFORT
OF YOUR CHAIR

What's the difference between Monopoly and tennis? Both are games, right? But one doesn't require you to stand up and the other demands you run around a court like a tornado. The same applies to brain games – they can be relatively inactive or incredibly active. Sometimes, as a dog owner, you're in sore need of the former. And that's okay. Maybe you're exhausted from a day at work or you're not physically able to run around. Never fear, there are brain games you can enjoy with your dog from the comfort of your chair.

BRAIN GAME: KOWTOW

Aim of the game: Teach your dog to bow to you. A bit of brain training and doggy yoga rolled into one. For this one, your dog will also need to be familiar with target training (see page 60).

1. With your dog standing in front of you (don't worry – you're still in your chair!), encourage them to target your hand with their nose.

2. Move your hand down slowly to between your dog's front paws. As long as they're sticking to what they've learnt in target training, your dog should follow your hand down and naturally put themselves into a bowing position – i.e. their head and front legs on the floor and their rear end in the air. As soon as they're in this position (don't wait too long in case they go into "flat"), reward them with a treat. It looks cute and makes you feel like royalty.

BRAIN GAME: SAY A LITTLE PRAYER

Aim of the game: Teach your dog the prayer pose. A fabulous game to play to impress your friends with how adorable your dog is.

1. With your dog sitting in front of you, hold a treat in front of their nose and move it upward so that they follow it. This should make your dog rise up, lifting their front paws until they rest on your forearm.

2. Once they're in this position and keeping their paws on your arm, lower the treat so your dog's head bows. It should look like they're deep in prayer. Reward them with treats from heaven!

3. As your dog gets the hang of it, introduce the words "Prayer time" as a cue for what's expected of them next. You'll also eventually be able to stop prompting, and they'll lower their head automatically.

BRAIN GAME: TIDY UP TIME

Aim of the game: Like living with kids, life with a dog can be untidy. So, if you're sitting in your chair looking around at a floor littered with dog toys, why not teach them to tidy up their own mess into a basket or box?

1. If your dog really isn't that untidy, simply spread a few of their toys around the floor. (They'll never know it was you.)

2. Begin by teaching what you mean by "put it away". Reward your dog for picking up one of their toys and then dropping it in a basket/box. Then to play the game, spread toys around a small area and point to each until your dog has put them all away.

3. To make the game more challenging, simply spread the toys over a wider area. Of course, if you're intent on staying in your chair, the toys will need to be close enough for you to point to!

QUICK WINS WITHOUT STANDING UP

Try these for easy and stimulating indoor games for your dog:

- Tug of war with a tough rope or a tug toy.

- Blow bubbles. Your dog will love chasing them.

- The shell game – a very simple problem-solving game. Let your dog watch as you put a treat under one of three cups. Shuffle the cups and let your dog find (and eat) the treat.

- Classic fetch. Just make sure it's something soft and harmless that you're throwing around your living room. You don't want a smashed TV screen or window.

GAMES
IN THE
GARDEN

Having some extra space means your dog can expend a bit more energy at the same time as stimulating their brain. The downside of being outside is that there are many distractions that are far more interesting to your dog than you are. Sad fact – their world doesn't actually revolve around you! You may find that you need to put more effort into keeping your dog focused – which will also require you to have more patience.

BRAIN GAME: OBSTACLE COURSE

Aim of the game: To encourage your dog to think about how it moves its body when faced with obstacles, as well as a great physical workout. Think agility training without having to run alongside worrying about a jiggling belly or not wearing your sports bra.

There are plenty of agility props to buy online or in pet stores, but there's no reason why you can't create your own. Jumps are easy to make using broom handles and you can fashion a simple tunnel by draping blankets over garden chairs. Use flower pots to create an obstacle for your dog to weave around, and steal a hula hoop from your kids for a perfect jumping obstacle.

Right – now you need to ignore what the book has told you about using treats as rewards to reinforce behaviour after the event rather than during it! To help your dog figure out what exactly it is they need to "do" with an agility course, you're going to need to bribe them and reward them.

Jumping hoops: Start off with the hoop low to the ground and entice your dog through with a treat. Even if the hoop is on the ground, reward them with the treat and lots of "well dones". Take it slowly, and gradually increase the height of the hoop – don't go too high too soon or you may put your wannabe gymnast off. Keep luring, keep rewarding. Before long – and if their little legs are long enough – they'll be jumping through hoops like circus acrobats.

Tunnel of love: Once they've got over their initial fears, most dogs love pelting through a tunnel. Encourage them to explore the tunnel initially by placing a few trusty treats in it (or shorten the length of the tunnel if they're really daunted). Once your dog is in, trot round to the other end and entice them through by calling and encouraging. They'll soon shift from gingerly edging their way through to running so fast they nearly take the tunnel with them.

Weaving: This is another easy brain exercise that aims to teach your dog to weave between obstacles. Line up any suitable items, leaving plenty of space for your dog to move between them. Using the magic treat, lure them through the first couple of obstacles and then let them feast on the treat as a reward. Then try the next two obstacles and reward again. Once your dog is used to zigzagging, you can drop the number of treats and only reward them when they're moved through all of the obstacles. The even more fun bit is encouraging your dog to weave and zigzag as quickly as possible. That will come with perseverance!

With an obstacle course, you're asking your dog to not only think but also to be super active. Unless you've got a very energetic and bouncy dog then you may find that an obstacle course doesn't keep a less active dog entertained for long. Every little bit helps though, so unless you're aiming for a national agility competition – which if you're reading this book you probably aren't – keep it at a pace your dog is happy with.

BRAIN GAME: TREASURE HUNT

Aim of the game: To bolster your dog's curiosity and stir their natural hunting instinct into action.

1. Get your dog into their sit or stay position. Once they're settled, present them with a treat and let them sniff it.

2. Keep your dog sitting while you hide the treat without them

seeing where – this could be the tricky bit, especially if you have a very nosey dog!

3. Give your dog the instruction to "find", and watch them run about manically until they finally pick up the scent of the treat and hone in on it.

4. Lavish them with praise and allow them to scoff the treat.

5. Repeat and hide in a different place each time. Make it trickier each time if you think your dog is up to it. This could involve them having to move something – for example, a plastic flower pot – in order to reach the treat.

BRAIN GAME: TOY ON A ROPE

Aim of the game: Take brain games on to another plane by hanging a toy up to thoroughly challenge your dog's motor and brain skills.

You'll need a bungee rope or similar that can be hung from something secure enough to support the weight of the rope being tugged. Firmly attach a toy (something that will withstand being tugged and pulled and, ideally, that you can stuff attractive treats inside). Adjust the height of the toy according to the size of your dog – you should start off at head height, then gradually raise the height as your dog gets adept at the game. (A Chihuahua might not get much fun from a toy hanging at the head height of a Great Dane!) Make sure you encourage your dog and praise them as they jump to reach the toy. They'll be flummoxed when the toy bounces back, but will learn to figure it out and anticipate the toy's reactions to their actions.

Use a sturdy toy that can withstand a fair amount of rough and tumble. However, do keep a careful eye on any damage to it that might harm your dog. Also, beware of any weather damage and decay if you leave the bungee cord and toy hung up outside.

OUT
WALKING

It can be hard to find time to play games with your dog in addition to what you would normally do on a day-to-day basis. Everyone has busy lives so don't feel guilty about that. There are ways to incorporate brain games into your daily walk that don't require you to be lugging lots of toys and props around with you. Don't let the thought that brain games need to be complicated put you off squeezing them in where you can. Jumping over logs and streams or zigzagging between fence posts are easy wins on a walk in the woods, for example.

BRAIN GAME: HIDE AND SEEK

Aim of the game: Make yourself the focus of your dog's attention and encourage them to find you. Just be warned that this game can be a bit awkward if there are lots of people around and you feel at all uncomfortable hiding by yourself behind a tree! Maybe one to save for those day when the park is quieter.

1. When your dog is distracted, make a beeline for a hiding place. Somewhere safe obviously, like behind a tree rather than in the middle of a roundabout. Don't go too far or you'll make it too hard for your dog, and make it somewhere you can still see to check if they're safe.

2. Call out their name – make finding you an exciting prospect, so sound excited! It'll take a few calls for them to track you to your exact spot, but when you are discovered, lavish your dog with praise.

3. The more you play this easy game, the quicker your dog will be able to find you and the less you'll need to call them (and draw attention to yourself as an adult hiding in a bush).

BRAIN GAME: FOLLOW THE LEADER

Aim of the game: A simple, no props game to keep your dog on its toes!

When you're out walking in an open space, try to walk in a different direction to that which your dog is taking. By changing your direction frequently and unexpectedly, they'll need to pay you very close attention. This is a really simple way to get their brain ticking and to stop them from being distracted.

BRAIN GAME: FAST, SLOW, STOP

Aim of the game: Like with Follow the leader (above), the aim here is to keep your dog's brain active as they have to pay close attention to you to know what's coming next rather than be in charge of the walk themselves.

While walking, say "faster" and increase your pace so that your dog must speed up to keep up. Next, say "slower" and decrease your pace. Then add in a "stop" command. Mix these up for some fun, and test how much attention your dog really is paying you. To be honest, they will think you've gone bonkers.

BRAIN GAME: SWITCH!

Aim of the game: To teach your dog to switch from one side of you to the other, while maintaining eye contact. It keeps your dog's attention on you, but it's also a useful trick for putting yourself between your dog and a potential issue, such as another dog or a tray of butcher's sausages.

1. Start off with your dog in a sitting position and use a treat to lure them to sit on your other side. If you're using a treat, then your dog will stay looking at you as they move.

2. Move on to starting your dog from a standing position, then at a slow walk and finally at your usual walking pace, introducing the "switch" command.

3. Once your dog has mastered this, they will be able to make swift switches and you'll add a new dimension of quick thinking and fun to their walk.

BRAIN GAME: TOUCH!

Aim of the game: To make a game of your dog exploring their environment and touching objects while out on your walk.

For this game, your dog will need to have had target training (see page 60), and be able to target items that you point to. During walks, use whatever command your dog is familiar with from target training to send them to touch the object that you indicate, for example a tree or a bench. If they touch the correct object then – as always – lavish them with praise (or treats if you're still in the early stages of learning this game).

QUICK TIPS TO MAKE YOUR DAILY WALK MORE STIMULATING

- Take different routes so that your dog doesn't get stuck in a rut. A new route will be full of exciting and unfamiliar things that your dog will love to explore with their senses.

- Take a toy or treats along which you can use as part of a treasure hunt. Let your dog seek them out to bolster that natural hunting instinct.

- Invite a fellow dog owner on your walk – providing their dog gets on with yours of course. A chance to play with another dog will teach your own dogs lots about how to interpret signals, and how to modify their own behaviour when interacting.

PROBLEMS

When you're outdoors, you'll find that brain games are liable to be disrupted by all of the distractions your dog encounters. Cyclists, joggers, wildlife, other dogs – all these conspire against you getting your dog's full attention. And this is why most of the games to play on your walk focus on encouraging your dog to keep their attention firmly on you! Stay patient, but be prepared for a doggy brain that goes off in tangents.

HOME
ALONE

As much as you love being with your dog, there are times – whether through work or other commitments – that you need to leave them home alone for a period during the day. You can make sure their food and drink needs are met while you are away and that the space they have is safe, but how do you stop them from getting bored and ripping up the furniture? If you'd like your beautiful home to remain intact and to keep your dog's brain stimulated while they're home alone, try some of these games.

BRAIN GAME: SCAVENGER HUNT

Aim of the game: Keep your dog's brain busy and their sense of smell entertained by making them hunt for food.

This is a fail-safe winner, and is guaranteed to appeal! Hide kibble or treats around the house in the areas where your dog is likely to spend time. They will have fun hunting it out while you're away. It can also create a really positive association for your dog because they'll be glad to see the back of you when you go out rather than worrying about it.

BRAIN GAME: SOLO FETCH

Aim of the game: For your dog to play fetch all by itself. Who needs a pesky human?

Make sure there's plenty of space for this game so that your house doesn't get turned upside down by an overexcited dog.

1. When your dog is watching, place a ball on a ramp (you may have to fashion this yourself – just make sure it's safe and secure) and let it roll down.

2. The next step is to employ your best reward-based training skills and teach your dog to drop the ball at the top of the ramp. They'll soon figure the fun in being able to drop and fetch by themselves. It will never replace the fun of outdoor fetch but it's a stimulating way to prevent boredom.

BRAIN GAME: BUCKET OF DELIGHTS

Aim of the game: To provide a treasure trove of fun for your dog to hunt through in pursuit of treats. Stimulates their senses and gives them a general feeling of excitement at being the Big Hunter.

Scatter some treats at the bottom of a sturdy bucket, then add a favourite toy. On top of that, place a towel or small blanket. Like making a doggy lasagna, continue to layer treats, toys and towels until the bucket is full. Leave it for your dog to explore and have a whale of a time with.

MORE TOP TIPS

- Leave a basket of toys for your dog to investigate. Be sure to change them regularly though, to keep things interesting, and add a new toy occasionally for an extra wow factor. Also, double check that all the toys are safe to leave with an unsupervised pet, for example that none of them are choking hazards.

- Leave the TV on. Believe it or not, there are actually channels aimed at providing boredom prevention for home-alone dogs. The world is a crazy place.

- If you don't want to leave the TV on, then just ensuring your dog can see out of a window is a fantastic way to keep their brain from stagnating. A lovely view out onto your garden will let them watch the world go by.

THE
CLASSICS

This is a serious book about how to brain train your dog, right? Partly. But it's also shown how it can be great fun for both you and your dog. So where would this book be without some of the classic tricks (sorry, brain games) that you can wheel out at parties and leave your family and friends in awe of your amazing training abilities? And, of course, your dog's unending patience and tolerance of you ...

BRAIN GAME: PLAY DEAD

Aim of the game: Cute rather than sinister, this tricky brain game teaches your dog to lie as still as a statue. Perfect for their next Hollywood audition.

1. Start off by getting your dog in a lying down/flat position. Use a treat to encourage them to turn their head to one side, and as they do, gently roll your dog onto its side. (This will take a few attempts for your dog to be comfortable with, so reward them every step of the way.)

2. Slowly extend the time your dog can stay lying in position. They'll figure out that they get more rewards for staying in position longer.

3. Once you've mastered the above position, introduce a hand signal that you can move to signal that your dog should roll onto its side. Gradually reduce the size of the hand movement needed for your dog to understand what it needs to do.

Just remember that it will be hard for your dog to lie completely still. If they're enjoying themselves then you're not going to be able avoid that wagging tail! You can also use this trick when your dog is tired and you want them to lie down and take a break.

BRAIN GAME: TIME FOR BED

Aim of the game: Teach your dog to lie down and cover themselves with a blanket. Another impossibly cute game that will get everyone saying "Awwww".

1. Spread out a blanket and ask your dog to lie on its side (see "Playing dead" above), with their legs pointing to the middle of the blanket. Practice, practice and reward.

2. At the same time, you need to teach your dog how to pick up the corner of the blanket, using a cue command such as "pick up" or "take". Again, give lots of rewards when they achieve this as fabric isn't easy for the dog to pick up with their mouth.

3. Time to combine step 1 and step 2. When your dog is in position lying down on the blanket, ask them to pick up the corner of it and then use your signal from "Playing dead" to indicate that they need to lie back down on their side. If your dog has managed to keep the blanket in its mouth, as it rolls onto its side, it will cover itself with the blanket. Hopefully!

This one is a difficult game, so have lots of patience and repeat endlessly to perfect it. It'll be worth the coos from your audience.

BRAIN GAME: SHAKE HANDS

Aim of the game: Simply teach your dog to shake hands with you. Another adorable trick, but far easier to master than "Playing dead" or "Time for bed".

1. Present your dog with a closed fistful of treats – they will automatically (because there's food!) use their paw to get at the treats as they realise they can't reach them with their mouth.

2. Introduce the cue word "Shake". Practice and repeat until your dog has mastered the connection between you putting out a hand and saying "Shake". You'll gradually be able to phase out actually having to hold smelly treats in your hand.

BRAIN GAME: SPINNING TOP

Aim of the game: Teach your dog to spin around. A simple game, but it looks impressive, and is an essential for dog/owner dance competitions.

1. Get your dog's attention with a treat, then hold it above your dog's nose and move it in a large circle above its head. The theory is that your dog should follow your hand – just keep trying it if they don't immediately.

2. Keep your hand moving and reward your dog if it follows your hand as it moves full circle.

3. Once your dog is spinning one full circle, add a verbal cue such as "spin" to introduce the association between the word and what you're expecting from your dog.

4. Gradually build up the number of spins your dog does before it earns the treat.

When your dog understands the hand movement plus cue word, you can phase out relying on a treat to set off the spinning.

Everyone thinks they have the best dog. And none of them are wrong.

W.R. PURCHE

No matter how little money and how few possessions you own, having a dog makes you feel rich.

LOUIS SABIN

DEALING WITH
SPECIFIC
PROBLEMS

ANXIOUS
DOGS

Not all dogs are the same. Each have their own personalities, and like humans, their own worries. If your dog is anxious, it may take a little longer for them to be comfortable with some of the games in this book. Perhaps your dog is new to your family, they are a rescue dog or their temperament is just timid and they're lacking in confidence. It doesn't mean you can't play games to keep them mentally stimulated – you just need to take a gentler approach and avoid scaring them.

TIPS FOR TRAINING AN ANXIOUS DOG

- Before doing any brain training with your dog, make sure they're completely relaxed and comfortable. They won't learn anything if they are stressed.

- Take the training slowly, even more slowly than usual. Don't overload your dog with new things, and learn to read their body language so you can tell when they're feeling anxious (see page 16).

- Keep your movements slow – too much enthusiasm may send your anxious dog running for cover.

- Try not to react to your dog's anxiety with nervousness. They'll pick up the signals and it can make their own mood spiral.

- If your dog does become anxious, try sitting next to them or stroking them to see if it helps reduce their anxiety. If it doesn't, don't crowd them or fuss around them – proceed to the step below ...

- Time out. Sometimes it's best to just abandon what you're doing together, and give your dog some quiet time to themselves, away from any stimulation.

BRAIN GAME: THE NAME GAME

Aim of the game: Teach your dog that their name has positive associations. This is particularly useful if your dog is shy when meeting people.

1. To get your dog excited about hearing their own name, start

by giving them a treat every time you say their name. This builds the positive association with their name.

2. The next step is only to give them the treat when they react to their name (and don't forget to give them lots of praise).

3. Eventually, phase out the treats. Try out your dog's reaction when a stranger calls them by their name. All being well, your dog will still make that positive association, regardless of whether they're familiar with the person. Do bear in mind though that this isn't a quick fix – anxious or shy dogs can take a long time to overcome their fear of meeting new people.

BRAIN GAME: A WHOLE NEW WORLD

Aim of the game: To encourage your dog to explore new things and not be afraid of them.

1. Surround your dog with a circle of new toys and unfamiliar objects – it really doesn't sound like you're being kind to them here, but bear with it!

2. Whenever they approach any of the items, reward them with a treat and praise.

3. Next time you play the game, introduce other new objects and repeat step 2. They will begin to build a positive association with unfamiliar things.

4. As your dog's confidence grows, you may notice their natural curiosity come out more when you're on walks. So if your dog is intent on exploring the tree stump they're previously shied away from, don't hold them back. Instead, reward them for their behaviour.

BRAIN GAME: STORY TIME

Aim of the game: Read to your dog to calm them down.

Dogs are increasingly used in schools as reading partners for children. Yes, reading to dogs can help children improve their reading skills! It also has the benefit of calming dogs down – and probably their owners too.

1. It's important that your dog stays close to you for this, so put them on a medium length leash. Get comfortable and read for 15 minutes. It doesn't matter what you read. Don't think that it has to be something that interests your dog – The Wind in the Willows will sound exactly the same to them as Fifty Shades of Grey.

2. If your dog is having trouble settling, just ignore them and carry on reading in a calm, even tone. Given a few minutes, your dog is likely to settle themselves. When they do, reward them and then keep reading. It's really important to reward calm behaviour – when your dog learns that such behaviour earns a reward, they will begin to calm themselves much more quickly, and without you having to try to make it happen.

3. Repeat this every day. You'll find that you're more well-read, and your dog has something to chat about with its canine pals next time you're out!

LESS ACTIVE AND
OLDER
DOGS

You've already found out how to keep your dog's brain busy when you're feeling the need to be stationary – see "From the comfort of Your chair", page 78. But what if your dog isn't able to bounce and run around like a crazy hound? Perhaps they've got an injury, are currently carrying too much weight or old age is starting to take a toll on their physical ability. This doesn't mean you shouldn't work on brain training with them – it can still have marvelous benefits. You just need to modify and slow things down.

Brain games for less active dogs don't need to be totally void of physical exercise. A very easy game is to simply spread some treats out in an area and allow your dog to snaffle them up. It's not complicated, but it does encourage your dog to get moving a little, and challenges them to use their sense of smell. Alternatively, fill a shallow box with crumpled newspaper and mix in some treats – perfect for your dog to forage through and explore. Senior or less active dogs never forget the thrill of the hunt.

YOU CAN'T TEACH AN OLD DOG NEW TRICKS?

Ah, that old – and inaccurate – adage. Of course you can; you just have to be more patient and accommodate your dog's limitations. Like humans, dogs' brains shrink as they age. But also like humans, dogs are never too old to benefit from positive mental experiences, and the prospect of a reward remains as attractive as ever. If your dog has developed hearing or sight problems, then of course that does makes things trickier. Rather than using visual cues to train them, you may have to use a tap on the shoulder instead. A dog with sore hips won't be up for games that involve sitting down. It's about finding work arounds.

In fact, it's easier to teach an older dog games and tricks as they can focus for longer than puppies. You'll need to accept that an older dog doesn't have the boundless energy of a pup anymore – but with positive reinforcement and patience, there's no reason why they can't outperform the young pretenders.

BRAIN GAME: NOSE BALANCE

Aim of the game: Exactly as you'd expect, teach your dog to balance a treat on their nose until you give them permission to eat it. Hardly any movement required at all and endlessly cute.

1. Start out with your dog sitting in front of you. Place a treat on their nose (you may find this challenging too until you find the best resting spot). When the treat has touched your dog's nose, remove it straight away, tell them to "take it" and let them eat it.

2. Keep on with the above, but gradually leave the treat in place for slightly longer each time. Lift a finger to signal that your dog should "wait". Then allow them to "take it" and enjoy the treat.

3. As your dog becomes practiced at staying very still and waiting for your signal, you can move further away from them and extend the length of the balance. Don't expect your dog to be tossing the treat up in the air and catching it in their mouth in an impressive feat of skill. It's most likely they'll simply let it drop to the floor before munching it. But that's no less of an achievement, so tell them so!

BRAIN GAME: DIG IT UP

Aim of the game: Give your dog a simple challenge to ignite their curiosity and sense of exploration.

1. Find a patch in your garden where the soil is loose and you're happy for your dog to dig. Bury a few toys, without making them too hard to get to.

2. Give your dog a hand by showing them a hint of what's hidden. They'll soon figure out that there's fun to be had retrieving the toys, and from being allowed to dig without being told off.

3. Don't expect your dog to keep digging for long if they

tire quickly. Any digging at all will give their front legs and shoulders a great workout without the stress put on their joints by running and jumping.

BRAIN GAME: MUFFIN TIN PUZZLE

Aim of the game: To hunt out treats under balls placed in a muffin tin. Challenges your dog's brain and stimulates both their sight and smell.

1. Start out by placing tennis balls in the dips in the muffin tin. I lide a treat under each ball.

2. Encourage your dog to understand what's going on by lifting up a ball, letting your dog see or smell the treat and then replacing the ball.

3. Your dog will figure out (quickly or slowly depending on them) how to knock a ball out to get the treat. Replace each ball without adding a new treat – this will encourage your dog to remember which balls don't have treats under them. Quite a challenge, but it will keep them busy!

A FEW EXTRAS ...

Try these other brain stimulating experiences that are perfect for a less active pooch:

- Target training – see page 60.

- The shell game – see page 81.

- Less active dogs still love a game of fetch – just don't throw the ball so far! If your dog has poor eyesight, buy a ball that has a bell in it, or makes a sound of some kind.

- If your dog is happy travelling in the car, go on a car ride. Let them see the world go by, and enjoy new sights and smelling new smells.

- Try to keep your dog involved in family activities generally – you may have to adapt a bit and make the activity less physical, but it will ensure your dog's brain keeps ticking. Don't let their world shrink just because they're getting older.

- Any games and puzzles that earn your dog treats will make them put their thinking cap on without requiring too much physical exertion.

HELP!
IT'S NOT
WORKING!

No one said brain training your dog would be easy. Every dog is different, and will react differently and learn at different rates. Stay patient and don't give up. Here are some of the most common problems and pitfalls, and how you and your dog can overcome them.

PROBLEM: MY DOG RUNS AWAY AND WON'T COME BACK

Fix it: Try keeping your dog on a long leash while introducing new games. They'll still have a sense of freedom but won't be able to run away from you.

PROBLEM: MY DOG ISN'T INTERESTED IN THE SLIGHTEST!

Fix it: Is your dog in the right frame of mind for playing? (See "Encouraging play", page 44.) There could be distractions competing for your attention so make sure you're in a calm, quiet environment that encourages your dog to focus solely on you.

If your dog is initially interested but becomes quickly distracted, keep the games short and don't do more than they can take in. If all still fails, try a different game – it could just be that your dog doesn't think that particular game is as exciting as you do.

PROBLEM: MY DOG JUST DOESN'T SEEM TO "GET IT"

Fix it: Consider your teaching methods. Are you being consistent? A dog won't learn unless they know exactly what is expected of them. If you keep changing the goalposts, they will just get confused and have no idea what to do. Make sure you're using consistent cue words and actions.

PROBLEM: MY DOG IS TOO FLIPPING EXCITED!

Fix it: If your dog always has an excessive amount of energy, then try and wear them out with a lot of physical exercise before you attempt brain training. Beware of completely exhausting them though or they won't be interested in playing. It's a fine line! If your dog's excitement is caused by anxiety, see page 105 for tips on how to calm them down.

PROBLEM: MY DOG WILL ONLY JOIN IN IF I LURE THEM WITH A TREAT

Fix it: Ah, you've confused rewards with bribery! Rather than rewarding your dog with a treat when they've done what you've asked of them, they think that you're rewarding the doing rather than the completing of the task. This isn't the end of the world, but you will need to help your dog unlearn this bad habit. Time, patience and starting from scratch is the answer.

PROBLEM: I'M SO EXASPERATED – NOTHING'S GOING RIGHT!

Fix it: First of all, keep calm. If you're getting stressed while doing brain games, your dog will immediately pick this up, their own stress will become heightened and they won't be able to learn. When you find yourself getting exasperated, take a few deep breaths and a short break. If that doesn't work, stop the game and try again tomorrow.

Are you getting too excited and overwhelming your dog? It could be that your tone when training is so outside your normal personality that your dog is freaking out about who this new person is. Keep your tone even and calm, and talk to your dog as you would normally.

If you're lacking confidence, your dog will pick up on your weakness. They're not being mean – it's their natural instinct as a predator. When embarking on anything new like brain training,

you're bound to feel a bit unsure. The key is practice – the more you train, the more your confidence will build and the less chance your dog will have to exploit you.

Intelligent dogs rarely want to please people whom they do not respect.

W.R. KOEHLER

TAKING IT TO THE
NEXT
LEVEL

NEXT STEPS: KEEPING YOUR DOG'S
BRAIN
STIMULATED

You and your dog have learnt lots of fantastic games and tricks. You've both really enjoyed it and your dog seems super healthy and happy (as do you). Brilliant – and a big "well done" to you both. But how do you keep up the momentum? Having played some of the games hundreds of times, do they become less stimulating and therefore less beneficial? The answer is no – any games you can do that keep your dog's body and brain active make a positive difference. However, there are ways to make sure that neither of you get bored and slip into inactivity:

- Mix it up. There will of course be games that become firm favourites for both you and your dog. That's fine – just don't forget those games that you tend to play less often. Revisit and recap what you've learnt. Not only does this keep things more interesting, it also ensures that brilliant skills your dog has learnt don't get forgotten. (The same applies to basic obedience training – well-worth going back to basics every so often.)

- Extend the challenge. You may have mastered a particular brain game, but is there a way you can make it just a little bit trickier and spice it up? Rather than balancing a treat on their nose, teach your dog to balance it on their paw (requires more stability). Try using six cups in the shell game rather than just three. Don't push your dog too hard or you could both get disheartened, but do try to make small, incremental changes that present an additional and stimulating challenge.

- Just add friends. If you have more than one dog, perhaps now's the time to introduce extra paws into the games! There are some pitfalls to this – see "Training more than one dog", page 47 – but if you're happy that your dogs are confident with their brain games, an additional pooch can add an extra dose of fun.

- Find somewhere new. If you tend to do all of your brain games in the same place, take the fun somewhere new. Dogs love new sights and smells, and it might be just what you need to freshen up your training sessions. Just be warned that you'll probably have to work a little harder to keep your dog's attention if they're easily distracted by unfamiliar things.

- Have a competition. If you know someone else who has been brain training their dog, get together for a bit of friendly competition. For example, see whose dog can complete a treasure hunt or obstacle course the fastest. Make sure the competition is healthy though – and that includes between you and the other owner!

- Get your children involved. Training your dog is down to the adults in the family, but once your dog is acclimatising to brain games, it's great fun to involve your children, too. Not only do they have more energy than you, it's really important they understand their pet and build a strong relationship with it.

- Make up your own brain games. You don't need to rely on books like this once you know the basics! When you've developed a good idea of the kind of games your dog enjoys most and you know what you're doing, invent your own or combine games you already know.

MY DOG
IS A GENIUS!

You've thrown yourself into brain training and your dog has mastered everything in a flash. Does this mean your dog is a genius?

Memory is an incredibly important part of how intelligent your dog is, and can be a general measure of whether you've got a hairy Einstein on your hands. If they have a good memory, they are likely to be able to learn more and absorb new things more quickly. Your dog's intelligence is not solely about memory though; you need to factor in how well they understand, think, communicate and problem solve.

There are – of course! – IQ tests that you can do with your dog. But is it worth IQ testing your dog? Probably not unless it's just for fun.

There can be downsides to having a really brainy dog. You'll have to work harder to keep them stimulated, and therefore stop the destructive behaviours associated with boredom creeping in. That can be exhausting for you as an owner, but it is absolutely necessary if you want your couch and curtains to remain in one piece.

If you really think your dog is a super canine genius, get involved in a dog owner's club where your pet can compete against other dogs and clubs. There are plenty of doggy sports to get involved with, such as agility, frisbee and owner–dog heelwork (that's dancing with your dog!). Before long, you might find yourselves on national TV in a talent competition.

CLEVER DOGS:
REAL-LIFE
STORIES

Dogs are clever beasts, there's no doubting that. Amazing sensory powers, intuitive, fast movers and fast learners. Here are some real-life stories to amaze and inspire you ...

THE NAVY DOG

In World War II, Bamse the Saint Bernard served aboard a Norwegian minesweeper. He became a legend in Scotland where the ship was stationed. He rescued one of the crew by diving into the sea and dragging him to safety. Bamse rescued another one who had been cornered by a knifeman by pushing the attacker into the sea. It was also said that when sailors got into fights, Bamse would stand with his paws on their shoulders in order to stop them.

THE MOUNTAIN RESCUE DOG

Another Saint Bernard, Barry, became famous in the early 1800s for saving 40 people's lives. His most famous rescue was that of a small child who had become trapped on a dangerous ice shelf. Barry reached the boy and kept him warm until rescue came. However, the rescue team were unable to reach them so the boy climbed onto the dog's back and Barry slowly dragged him to safety.

AMAZING GUIDE DOGS

The service that guide dogs provide to their companions is incredible. They're a wonderful example of how specialist training can achieve so much. None more so than when 61-year-old Cecil Williams fainted on a subway platform and fell onto the tracks. After having tried to tug his blind owner away from the edge, guide dog Orlando leapt down onto the tracks with his owner and tried to wake him up by licking and kissing him. Miraculously, both survived a train rolling over the top of them.

DOCTOR DOG

Dogs have been revered and feared over the centuries for their ability to foretell an earthquake, volcano eruption or other natural disaster, and more recently for their ability to detect illness in humans. In 1989, a Border Collie/Doberman Pinscher mix relentlessly sniffed and nipped at a single mole on her owner's leg, but not at any of the other moles. The one that attracted the dog's attention turned out to be malignant.

WILDLIFE WARRIORS

Sniffer dogs are amazing – they work their sensory magic for locating drugs, missing people and incendiary devices, just to name a few examples. (Did you know that your dog can hear with each ear independently? This gives them the ability to listen to two different sounds at once and to filter sounds – one of the reasons dogs are great at search and rescue.) Sniffer dogs are now being used by WWF and the Kenya Wildlife Service to tackle the illegal wildlife trade. Air is suctioned out from shipping containers, filtered and then presented to the dogs. Using their amazing sense of smell, the dogs can sniff out even the tiniest amounts of ivory, rhino horn and other illegal products.

THE WAR HERO

In 1917, a stray dog wandered onto the Yale college campus, in Connecticut, where members of the military were in training to fight World War I. The soldiers called him Stubby and smuggled him to the front lines in France. While there, Stubby warned soldiers of gas attacks and helped locate injured soldiers. Stubby was given the rank of sergeant for attacking a German spy.

RECORD BREAKERS

- Sweet Pea, an Australian shepherd/border collie mix holds the world record for the fastest 100 metres completed with a can balanced on her head. She completed the feat in a time of 2 mins and 55 secs.

- Norman the Scooter Dog holds the record for the fastest 30 metres completed by a dog on a scooter. He did the dash in just 20.77 seconds. He can also ride a bike …

- The current record holder for balloon popping by a dog is Twinkie, a Jack Russell terrier, who managed to pop 100 balloons in 39.08 seconds.

THE
FUTURE

As with everything else in our fast-paced world, brain training your dog isn't immune to the relentless march of technology. Let's for the moment assume that in 10 years' time you've still got a real dog and not one fashioned from metal and circuits. And that you will still need to train your dog rather than simply input a programme. At least with a robot dog you'd save on poo bags!

Interestingly, brain training is already ahead of the game, and you – the dog owner – are fast becoming redundant. If your dog is home alone and you've got cash to splash, then you and your pampered pet could benefit from the following:

- Cameras connect to an app, letting you see what your dog is doing, and allowing you to speak to it and take photos to upload to social media.

- Automatic ball launchers – yes, really. For those dogs who really can't be without a game of fetch. You can even train your dog to reload it themselves.

- An activity monitor that tracks your dog's movement and sleep, and records the stats on your phone.

- Treat dispensers that you can operate remotely via your phone.

And these days, you don't even have to physically participate in brain training apart from to switch on your electronic device. Austrian cognitive biologists have trialed touchscreen apps as a way of keeping elderly dogs mentally active and countering decline in memory. While it took the dogs a while to learn how to use the apps, once they could, they had a whale of a time playing the equivalent of dog sudokus.

But it's not just limited to older dogs. You can download apps for your dog (and the ones for cats work equally well) that require them to participate by licking the screen (anti-bacterial wipes at the ready!) or by touching it with their paw or nose. Whatever next? Sometimes it's best not to try to imagine. What we do know is that dogs will always need and benefit tremendously from the love and attention that their owners can give them. That is something that will never change.

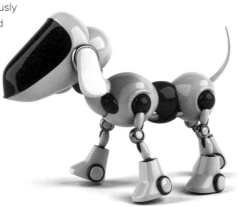

I can train any dog in 5 minutes. It's training the owner that takes longer.

BARBARA WOODHOUSE